Jackie,

You have truly been a blessing in my life. Thanks for all your help & understanding you've shown me & may God continue to bless you on a daily basis.

Love ya.
Wendi

3-11-95

"One can never say enough about faith.
Pamela Reeve's classic is poignant yet powerful—
she fills each page with fresh,
new definitions for our faith in the Lord Jesus."

"Without faith you can't please God.
With it, you can move mountains.
Pamela Reeve cuts to the heart of what it means
to trust God."

"Faith is...
not pious thoughts or good feelings about God
but daily choices,
spelled out simply, lucidly, practically,
in Pamela Reeve's little gem of a book."

Dedicated
To Jesus, the author
and finisher of our faith.

Faith Is...

Pamela Reeve

Illustrations by Gwen Babbitt

MULTNOMAH BOOKS · SISTERS, OREGON

Faith Is. . .
©1994 by Pamela Reeve
Illustrations © Gwen Babbitt
Published by Multnomah Books
a part of the Questar Publishing Family
Edited by Larry R. Libby   Designed by David Uttley
Printed in the United states of America
International Book Standard Number 0-88070-691-0

For Information:
Questar Publishers, Inc., Post Office Box 1720, Sisters, Oregon 97759

Reeve, Pamela.
        Faith Is. . ./Pamela Reeve.
            p.   vm
ISBN 0-88070-622-8: $12.99
1. Faith--Meditations.   2. Meditations.   I. Title.
BV4637.R44   1994   94-11231
242'.723--dc20   CIP

        94 95 96 97 98 99 00 01 — 10 9 8 7 6 5 4 3 2 1

A Note from the Author

*. . . ceasing to worry,
leaving the future to the God
who controls the future.*

*I*t wasn't a familiar mood, but I was depressed—way down—
and I knew it. I'd been Dean of Women at Multnomah Bible
College for four years. My life and ministry, as I looked back,
seemed unproductive. Full of mistakes. Futile.
I drove out into the country and sat down on a grassy river bank
to do some thinking. As I sat, a verse of scripture pierced my
thoughts. It was the Lord's words to Abraham in Genesis 12:3.

"In you all the nations of the earth will be blessed."

I remembered reading somewhere that blessing
springs from faith.

"Bless the nations?" I laughed at the thought.
"Lord, I can't bless fourteen acres of Multnomah campus."
Immediately countering that thought it was as if God
said to me, "Will you believe your feelings...
or my Word?" Then, He gave me the faith to say
"Lord, I will believe you."
And He kept developing my faith. I began writing down what
faith meant to me. One year I decided to make a Christmas gift
for a missionary friend.
I used my "Faith Is" statements written in
calligraphy and ended up with a colorful little book to send. One
went to Taiwan, another to Zaire, another to a former student in
South America. Then God's hand began to work.
From around the world I heard people tell me how "Faith Is"
had encouraged them. And the Lord reminded me of that
promise on the riverbank years ago.
Since that first hand-made book, more than a million copies of

"Faith Is" have been sold worldwide.

Twenty-five years have passed since I wrote those first statements of faith. For this new edition I have added some new expressions of faith that reflect my own journey as my knowledge of self and my deep need of God have grown. They have also been forged by entering into the lives of today's young men and women who are coming out of a deteriorating society with its corrupting influences, fractured homes, and deep wounds. Faith now manifests itself in new contexts. Yet the living God is able to meet any need, quench any thirst, heal any wound. For all times and conditions, faith in the God of deliverance is the secret of triumph in the Christian life.

"Faith is...
resting in His love,
His presence,
His provision."

PAMELA REEVE

. . . The conviction of realities
I cannot see
or feel.

"Let us fix our eyes on Jesus,
the author and perfecter of our faith,
who for the joy set before him endured the cross,
scorning its shame, and sat down
at the right hand of the throne of God."

HEBREWS 12:2

. . . Not a leap in the dark
nor
a mystical experience
nor
an indefinable encounter
with Someone. . .

but
trust in One who has
explained Himself in a Person—
Christ,
in an historical
record—the Bible.

... The handle by which I take
God's promises
and apply them to
my
particular problems.

...Remembering
I am indispensable
to GOD
when I feel I only clutter up
the landscape.

*...Allowing God
to straighten the record
when
false things have been said
about me.*

"Be on your guard;
stand firm in the faith; be men of courage;
be strong."

1 CORINTHIANS 16:13

*. . . Doing the right thing
regardless of the consequences,
knowing God will
turn
the ultimate effect to good.*

Faith Is...

. . . Confidence in God
when money is
running out,
not
rolling in.

...Remembering
that in the kingdom of God
everything is based
on promise,
not
on feeling.

*. . . Rejecting
the feeling of panic
when things seem
out of control.*

...Refusing
the thinking that God
loves and cherishes the popular,
attractive, talented Christian
more than He loves and cherishes
plain me.

...Remembering
I am God's
priceless treasure
when I feel
utterly worthless.

... Realizing what God is going to
do through me will be on the basis
of miracle
not
man power, His promise
not
my goodness.

"We live by faith, not by sight."

2 CORINTHIANS 5:7

... Expecting God
to accomplish miracles
—through insignificant
me
with my five loaves
and two fishes.

. . . Dependence
on God to work
miracles
in my disposition.

... Thanking God for
the specific thing
that upsets me.

Faith Is...

...Committing
loved ones' problems
to God to solve.

. . . Recognizing that God is the LORD of TIME when my idea of timing doesn't agree with His.

*. . . The assurance
that God is perfecting
His design for me
when my life's course, once a
swift-flowing current,
seems a stagnant pool.*

. . . Confidence in God's faithfulness
to me
in an uncertain world,
on an uncharted course,
toward an unknown
future.

"For we are God's workmanship,
created in Christ Jesus to do good works,
which God prepared in advance
for us to do."

EPHESIANS 2:10

. . . Reliance on the certainty
that God has a
pattern
for my life
when everything seems
meaningless.

. . . Resting in the fact
that God has an
objective
in leaving me on the scene
when I feel
useless to Him
and a burden to others.

. . . Expecting
a sea of golden grain from the
bleak, barren, endless fields—
watered only by my tears—
where I walk alone.

"Consider it pure joy, my brothers,
whenever you face trials of many kinds,
because you know that the testing of your faith
develops perseverance."

JAMES 1:2-3

...Claiming God's strength
to accept and endure
weariness,
pain,
decline
—patiently.

. . . Depending on the fact that
God is love,
not on my ability to figure out
WHY, in the midst of
smashed hopes,
reversal, tragedy.

Faith Is...

...Confidence
that God is acting
for my highest good
when He answers
"NO"
to my prayers.

. . . Thanking God
when I am left with
shattered plans,
that He has
better plans.

. . . *Rejoicing in the eternal glory*
accumulating from my
temporary troubles
when my usefulness or health
or loved one
is gone
and I feel "not needed."

Faith Is...

. . . Refusal to worry
when I haven't a clue
as to what God
would have me do
with my life.

...Appreciating that my capacity to
feel, communicate, think,
achieve, choose, create, and
commune with God
comes from His making me
like Himself.

...Acknowledging God
as the giver
of abilities
when success is mine.

... Thanking God for His gift
of emotional health,
not assuming
it all stems from my ability
to cope with life.

"These have come so that your faith —
of greater worth than gold,
which perishes even though refined by fire —
may be proved genuine
and may result in praise, glory, and honor
when Jesus Christ is revealed.

1 PETER 1:7

...Something God will
prove genuine
by
testing.

...Standing on the fact that God
has designed me flawlessly
for His purposes in the universe
when I feel
everything about me is
one big mistake.

...Developed through hardship
disappointment, disillusionment,
conflict, frustration, failure,
loss—
not through stained glass
nor sweet religious props.

"And now these three remain:
faith, hope, and love.
But the greatest of these
is love."

1 CORINTHIANS 13:13

...Fantasy-like, unless
it is made real
in the way I interact
with people.

. . . Cooperating with God
in changing me,
rather than taking refuge in
piously
berating myself.

Faith Is...

...Not related to my believing
hard enough, nor my
emotional exhilaration or flatness,
but rests on
what God guarantees
in His Word.

*"Consequently, faith comes
from hearing the message, and the message is heard
through the word of Christ."*

ROMANS 10:17

...Not faith in faith itself,
but faith in the
— FACTS of Scripture
— FACT of Christ's death
— FACT of His resurrection.

"He who did not spare his own Son,
but gave him up for us all —
how will he not also, along with him,
graciously give us all things?"

ROMANS 8:32

. . . Not an idea that God is
somehow trustworthy,
but confidence in Him based on His
proof of utter trustworthiness
in dying for me.

...Not a vague hope
of a happy hereafter,
but
an assurance of heaven based on
my trust in Christ's death
as payment for my sins.

. . . Refusing to feel guilty over
PAST confessed sins, when
God, the Judge,
has sovereignly declared me—
"PARDONED."

"For I know the plans I have for you,"
declares the Lord, "plans to prosper
you and not to harm you,
plans to give you hope
and a future."

JEREMIAH 29:11

. . . Ceasing to worry, leaving the
FUTURE
to the God who
controls the future.

...Realizing that God is the
God of NOW,
carrying on His purposes in every
tedious, dull, stupid,
boring, empty
minute of my life.

Part Two

New expressions on the journey of faith

Faith Is...

...Remembering I stand
blameless before God
where I see nothing but my own
meanness,
pettiness,
selfishness.

*. . . Resting in the fact
that I am not
on probation with God.*

...Accepting the ordinary
as God's best
for me when I want
to be special.

. . . Trusting God to satisfy
when I am weaning myself
from unhealthy but enjoyable
pacifiers: workaholism, perfectionism,
fantasy life,
overly dependent relationships.

"If we confess our sins,
he is faithful and just and will forgive us our sins
and purify us from all unrighteousness.

1 JOHN 1:9

. . . Remembering the fact that
though I feel self-condemned,
over confessed sin,
GOD NOW HAS NOTHING
AGAINST ME.

*...Accepting the truth
that in spite of the wreckage
I've caused and grieve over,
God, who has wiped the slate clean,
delights in me.*

...Giving up that image
of perfection
I struggle for—
accepting
GRACE.

...Seeing that though I may always
live with scars from healed
wounds of the past,
God
has incorporated them into
His perfect plan for my life.

...Realizing
that I am useful to God
not
IN SPITE of my scars
but
BECAUSE of them.

Faith Is...

. . . Trusting God's final outcomes
when all I'd dreamed of
for my loved one
is shattered.

...Having confidence that God will
take the bad choices
others have made that affect me
and use them for my
ultimate good.

"*Now faith is being sure of what we hope for and certain of what we do not see.*"

HEBREWS 11:1

Faith Is...

. . . Resting in the fact
that though life is not fair,
the Righteous Judge says
He will settle all accounts fairly,
eternally in heaven.

...Clinging to Christ for grace to
resist
when I am keenly tempted,
knowing He has endured the same,
has tender compassion
on my weakness,
and will help me stand strong.

Faith Is...

...Knowing
that it is not
what I am doing
but
what He is doing in me
that really matters.

eighty-three

. . . Ceasing from forever trying
to make myself good enough
for God
and letting Jesus
really
be my Savior.

. . . Realizing that feeling totally
inadequate, weak, needy, empty is
not
the worst that can happen
to me but the best.
The kingdom belongs to
the poor in spirit.

"By faith Abraham, when God tested him,
offered Isaac as a sacrifice.
He who had received the promises was about to
sacrifice his one and only son…
Abraham reasoned that God could raise the dead,
and figuratively speaking, he did receive
Isaac back from death."

HEBREWS 11:17, 19

...Letting go of that
which God is asking me for.

...Believing He,
the miracle worker, can turn
my stone-cold indifference into
a fire of love
toward certain "unlovables."

...Accepting the fact
that the way to Him
is through His divesting me
of all sense of my goodness
and leaving me with
His alone.

*. . . Remembering that God loves me
as tenderly and fervently
when I fail—
as when I am walking
uprightly.*

...The heavenly country
He has opened for me to enjoy
and the river of
His love
that flows down to me.

"Since, then, you have been raised with Christ,
set your hearts on things above,
where Christ is seated at the right hand of God.
Set your minds on things above,
not on earthly things."

COLOSSIANS 3:1,2

*. . . Not trying to turn this howling
wilderness called life into a garden
of fountains and flowers,
but daily
fixing my heart and mind
on Christ. . .*

. . . Realizing
God is not disillusioned
with me, having known
when He chose me
all I'd ever do
or think.

...Marveling in the fact
that nothing less
than the Shekhinah glory
of God's presence
dwells in me,
His temple.

"Without faith
it is impossible to please God,
because anyone who comes to him must believe
that he exists and that he rewards those
who earnestly seek him.

HEBREWS 11:6

. . . Recalling that I grow
not by trying,
but by trusting.

*. . . Not faith in my "devotions"
or "spiritual disciplines"
but in God.*

...Remembering
that though my way
is dark as night to me,
GOD can see
and guides me
unerringly.

ninety-nine

"You shall have no other gods
before me.
EXODUS 20:3

*...Moving from worshipping
at my own shrine
to God's.*

...Accepting His gift
of unchanging love
without trying
to make myself
worthy of it.

...Not expecting
anything
from myself,
but expecting
everything
from God.

...Not trust
in my religious performances,
but
in Christ's performance
for me.

...Accepting the fact
that God controls my
spiritual growth when above all else
I want to be in charge of
that area.
Must I be THAT dependent?

"Do everything without complaining or arguing,
so that you may become blameless and pure,
children of God without fault in a crooked and
depraved generation, in which
you shine like stars in the universe..."

PHILIPPIANS 2:14, 15

...Waiting patiently for God
to make me more Christ-like
through
people and circumstances
when I want Him to give me
a quick fix
—preferably painless.

. . . Believing in the midst of
suffering and need
that God will be enough,
that He will enable me
to make it through.

*...Remembering
that the "saint"
who drives me crazy
is indwelt by God
and precious to Him.*

"The only thing that counts is faith
expressing itself through love."

GALATIANS 5:6b

*...Understanding
my "experiences with God"
won't cause a fraction of an inch
of spiritual growth
unless they are hammered out
in daily relationships.*

... Presenting my raw neediness
to God in utter dependence
on Him to produce in me
His life of Purity, Patience,
Perseverance, Humility,
Love.

...Accepting that God's work
has made me
clean, clean, clean!
When my basic concept
of myself is
soiled, dirty, defiled.

"Because you are my help,
I sing in the shadow of your wings."

PSALM 63:7

*. . . Remembering I carry
God's awesome presence
into each daily routine encounter
when I feel like a
dull leaden weight.*

. . . Believing that the persevering,
seemingly unanswered prayer
of many years
is not an exercise in futility
but the means by which God is
accomplishing His great
eternal purposes—in His time.

. . . Keeping on keeping on
when I am dog-tired, discouraged,
disillusioned, deserted,
dusty dry—
cast on His strength
alone.

*...Accepting the fact
that God knows better
than I do
what is ultimately good
for me.*

...Depending on God's
enablement
to live and be blessed
in a fallen world
rather than insisting
He change it.

"Do not be anxious about anything,
but in everything, by prayer and petition,
with thanksgiving, present your requests to God."

PHILIPPIANS 4:6

. . . Daily having part
in the thrill of our times—
the greatest global gathering
of people into the kingdom of God
the world has ever seen—
through prayer.

Faith Is...

...Living
with the
unexplained.

*. . . Hanging onto God
while confronting in love,
at the risk of rejection.*

*... Trusting that I will become
more loving and patient,
not by my strenuous effort,
but by trusting His life in me
to produce those qualities.*

Faith Is...

. . .Accepting servanthood rather
than pushing your way
to the top.

...*"So that Christ may dwell in
your hearts through faith. And I pray that you,
being rooted and established in love,
may have power, together with all the saints,
to grasp how wide and long and high and deep is
the love of Christ..."*

EPHESIANS 3:17, 18

. . . Realizing
the thing God wants
from me is simply
letting Him
love me.

. . . Entering spiritual warfare
with the confidence
of being on the
Victor's side.

...Engaging in the deepest joy
of heaven
knowing His unfathomable love
for me
as I walk through the
thorny desolate NOW.

. . . Realizing
I am the treasure
Christ sought
and found
and that I am His joy.

Faith Is...

...Knowing my sins
have not only been paid for,
but taken away from me,
never
to be seen again.

"I have been crucified with Christ
and I no longer live,
but Christ lives in me. The life I live in the body,
I live by faith in the Son of God,
who loved me and gave himself for me."

GALATIANS 2:20

...Drawing comfort
from the knowledge
that when I weep,
He weeps with me.

Faith Is...

...Living the consciousness that I
dwell beyond the grave,
beyond the farthest star, hid with
Christ in the heart of God, in the
center of His overwhelming love
as I walk through this scene
of toil, tears, and tempests.

...Glorying in the fact
that I am pure
because He is pure
and we two
are one.

_. . . Turning to God in my pain,
not using people,
things, activity,
to deaden it._

*. . . Praising God
through my tears
when my sun
is eclipsed.*

*"On that day you will realize that I
am in my Father,
and you are in me, and I am in you."*

JOHN 14:20

*. . . Delighting in the fact
that though I am a vessel
marred, unsightly, broken,
I am filled
by God's own hand
with Christ, His treasure.*

. . . Walking before God,
not
before my friends.

. . . Trusting that God is
doing His work in me when I feel
inwardly cold, hollow, lifeless,
deserted, and
I long for reassuring feelings.

...Letting go of my demands
that another change
and
looking to God for the changes
He sees I need.

... Trusting His limitless strength
when I realize
I am powerless to accomplish
anything of value.

*. . . Drawing on God's grace
to help others succeed
where I have failed.*

*. . . Resisting the temptation
to take back
into my own hands
that which I have given to God
to control.*

"Then we will no longer be infants, tossed back and
forth by the waves, and blown here and there by
every wind of teaching and by the cunning and
craftiness of men in their deceitful scheming.
Instead, speaking the truth in love, we will in all
things grow up into him who is the Head,
that is, Christ."

EPHESIANS 4:14, 15

. . . Speaking the truth in love
even at the cost of
position
or relationship.

. . . Taking my eyes off
my good self,
or my bad self,
or my wounded self,
and keeping them on Himself.

*...The dependence
of a newborn.*

. . . Remembering He has said
I am PRECIOUS
in His sight,
His beloved.

...Living in anticipation
of heaven where He
the Bridegroom
watches and waits for me.

*... Realizing
I am the treasure Christ sought
and found
and that I am His joy.*

. . . Remembering that much
about me will change in heaven,
but I'll never be one bit
more righteous than I am
RIGHT NOW.
Christ is my righteousness.

"But as for me, it is good to be near God.
I have made the Sovereign Lord my refuge;
I will tell of all your deeds."

PSALM 73:28

... Remembering in the midst
of my heartache
that nothing can change
my greatest blessing,
His presence with me.

. . . Remembering that much
about me will change in heaven,
but I'll never be one bit
more righteous than I am
RIGHT NOW.
Christ is my righteousness.

... Waiting on God
to give me the greatest joy
on earth —
the experience of His love.

"I have fought the good fight,
I have finished the race,
I have kept the faith."

2 TIMOTHY 4:7

. . . The WAY
to please God.

*. . . The conviction:
The Promiser keeps
His promises.*